Experience HENDRIX

BOOK ONE—BEGINNING GUITAR METHOD

EXPERIENCE HENDRIX
"A JIMI HENDRIX FAMILY COMPANY"

Distributed by

MUSIC SALES LIMITED

http://www.jimi-hendrix.com

Credits

Author: Michael Johnson

Cover Photography: Nona Hatay

Inside Illustration Photography: Terri Giago

Book Design/Production: Rebecca Geisler

Editing: Terri Giago, John Jansen, and Aubbie

TABLE OF CONTENTS

Quick Start
Follow the pick icons if you want to start playing right away. It's strongly suggested that you go back and review the pages you skipped to gain the full benefits this book has to offer.

ANATOMY OF THE GUITAR

QUICK START

Electric

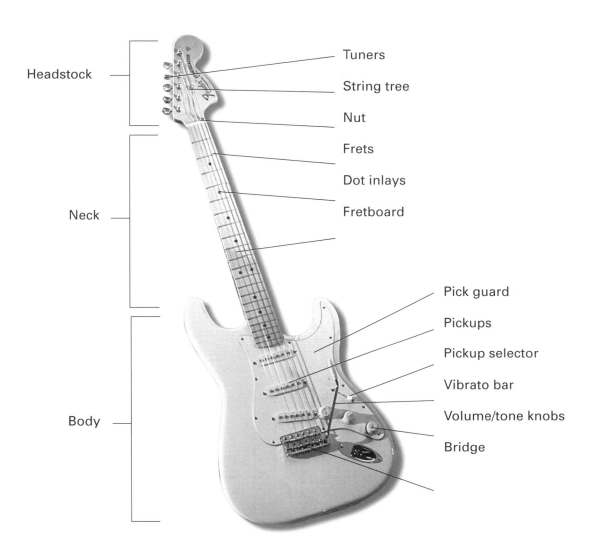

Headstock

Neck

Body

Tuners

String tree

Nut

Frets

Dot inlays

Fretboard

Pick guard

Pickups

Pickup selector

Vibrato bar

Volume/tone knobs

Bridge

*Fender "Woodstock" Stratocaster, courtesy of
Fender Musical Instrument, Inc.*

GUITAR HEALTH

It is very important to have an instrument that is in good playing condition. Have a reputable guitar repairman or luthier (guitar builder) evaluate the instrument to see if your guitar is in good shape. This will save you many hours of frustration.

GUITAR	DEFINITION	PROBLEM
Tuners	The tuning pegs of the headstock.	Poor tuner condition can make it difficult to keep the guitar in tune.
Nut condition	The height of the grooves in the nut.	Worn grooves can cause string buzzing.
Fret condition	The worn or chipped condition of the frets.	Worn frets can cause playing difficulty and buzzing.
Truss rod	The metal rod that runs through the length of the neck to support it and keep it from warping or bowing.	Incorrect adjustment of truss rod can cause the frets to buzz and make it difficult to press the strings to the fretboard.
Neck condition	The straightness/cracking of the neck.	A warped neck can cause buzzing noises and tuning problems.
String gauge	The size of the set of strings on the guitar.	Acoustic and heavy gauge strings can be difficult to play at first.
Action	The distance of the string from the fretboard.	If the action is set too high the strings can be difficult to press down. Too low can cause buzzing.
Electronics	The guitar pickup, knobs, switches, jacks, and wiring.	Some indications of needed electronic maintenance: crackling, buzzing, humming, and feedback.
Body condition	The condition of the parts of the guitar body.	Cracking in the body structure can affect the condition of the neck and bridge.
Bridge	The anchor of the guitar strings to the guitar body.	An incorrectly set bridge can cause buzzing, poor action, and tuning problems.
Vibrato bar	The bar attached to a floating bridge used to drop or raise the pitch of all the strings in unison. This bar is used as an effect.	A vibrato bar can make it difficult to tune the guitar. For your first guitar try to purchase an instrument without the bar or have a repairman set it up with extra springs and maximum resistance.
Sound-board bracing (acoustic)	The bracing that supports the back and top of the body interior of an acoustic guitar.	Loose soundboard bracing can cause buzzing of the guitar body and the raising of the top of the soundboard.

BASIC SITTING & STANDING POSITION

Sitting

Position the guitar so that your leg supports the guitar body.

NOTE: younger or smaller people may need to adjust, either by sitting in a smaller chair or raising their leg using a book(s).

Standing

Position the guitar strap to hold the guitar body in a comfortable mid-body position. Your right hand should rest comfortably over the bridge of the guitar; your left hand should support the neck.

HAND POSITIONS

Hands

The fingers on your hands are numbered from pointer finger to pinkie, 1-4. The thumb is labeled "T".

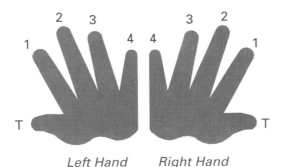

Left Hand   *Right Hand*

Thumbs

Position your hand underneath the neck with the fingertips on the fretboard. Place your THUMB VERTICALLY on the back of the neck to help support your fingers to press firmly on the guitar neck. Do not collapse your thumb.

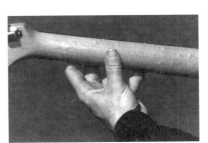

Correct

Fretting

Press your fingers firmly down on the desired strings. Make sure you apply enough pressure on the string to avoid a buzzing noise. Always place the fingers directly behind the metal frets, not on them, to ensure you get the proper sound.

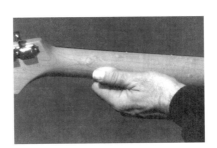

Incorrect

Your thumb can also be used as a tool to play notes by wrapping it around the top of the neck. This technique was often used by Jimi both for playing notes on the lower strings and for support in bending strings

HAND POSITIONS *(continued)*

Building Hand and Finger Strength

Building up the strength of your hand and fingers is a critical element of playing guitar. There are several exercises you can do:

1. Squeeze a hand grip.
2. Squeeze a tennis ball.
3. Isometric: Over-squeeze your fingers on your thumb.
4. Isometric: Over-press your fingers on the fretboard.
5. Isometric: Make a fist and squeeze firmly.
6. Isometric: Press your fingers together on both hands.
7. Practice the guitar!!!

Holding the Pick

To hold the pick properly, pinch the pick between your thumb and 1st finger, positioning your thumb horizontally across the pick and your 1st finger vertically down the pick or curled in slightly.

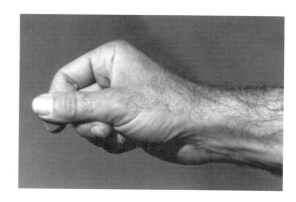

Position of Picking Hand

It is important for your picking hand to make contact with the guitar body while picking. There are two methods of achieving this:

1. Position the palm of your hand against the bridge of the guitar. (Do not mute the strings by touching the strings on the bridge.)

2. Position your 4th finger on the guitar body just below the strings. (Be sure you clear the strings with your hand to avoid muting them.)

Fingernails

Since you use the tips of your fingers to press the strings, short fingernails are a must!

Calluses

Your fingertips will be very tender at first. Don't worry, calluses will develop the more you practice.

GUITAR GRID & GUITAR NECK BASICS

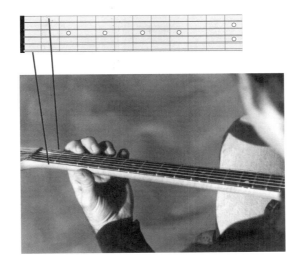

Here is an example of the right-handed guitar grid that we will use throughout this book.

Grid is from the view of the player.

For Lefties

Left handed guitars are available in music stores. To use this book, left-handed players can mentally mirror the right handed grids (see illustration below).

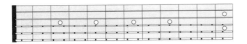 

If you are still having difficulty converting this grid to left-hand, try standing this book vertically on end and placing a mirror at an angle so that you can view the grid through the mirror. Eventually, you will be able to convert these grids mentally.

Page   Mirror

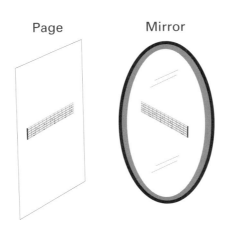

Guitar Neck

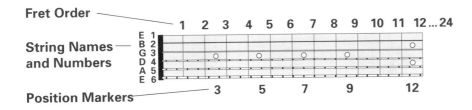

Fret Order—The frets are numbered starting with 1 after the nut, up to 21 (24 for some electric guitars).

String Names and Numbers—The strings are numbered 1-6, starting with the little string (E).

Position Markers (also called Inlays or Dot Markers)—The position markers are placed for quick reference of your position on the guitar neck. They are generally placed on the 3rd, 5th, 7th, 9th, 12th (double dotted to show octave), 15th, 17th, 19th, and 21st frets—but this spacing may be different for some guitars.

Jimi Hendrix preferred using right-handed guitars, restringing them upside down so that he could play left-handed. This gave him easy access to the volume control and vibrato bar, enhancing his unique style and sound.

Here is a catchy phrase that you can use to memorize the order of the string names:

(1) **E**aster
(2) **B**unnies
(3) **G**et
(4) **D**own
(5) **A**t
(6) **E**aster

TUNING METHODS

It is important to have a good reference when tuning your guitar. If not, the guitar may be tuned to itself, but out of tune with other instruments. This can make it difficult to play along with a CD, tape, or other musicians.

Note: It is important to check your tuning occasionally while you are playing.

Tuning to the Accompanying CD

This recording contains all of the correct notes for each of your open guitar strings. This tuning method is described on CD.

Electronic Tuners

For beginners, I strongly suggest purchasing an electronic tuner. The advantage is that you can actually see, on the tuning indicator, when your guitar is correctly tuned. Tuners can be used as a tool to help you develop your own "ear."

Pitch Pipe

A pitch pipe is a lot like a harmonica, but each note is specifically set for each string of the guitar. This is a great tool for pitch reference.

Tuning by Keyboard (price varies)

The keyboard can be used to find the correct note for each of your guitar strings. See illustration of which notes to use on the keyboard.

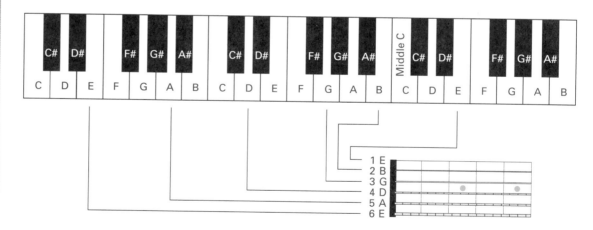

Tuning Fork

A common method for tuning the guitar is to use an "E 329.63Hz" tuning fork. When struck, this instrument resonates a pitch with which you can tune your open "E" string. After setting the "E" string you can tune the remaining strings by using the fretboard tuning method shown here.

Tuning on the Fretboard

Once you have tuned the 6th string (E) to a reference note using one of the methods above, you can tune the remaining strings by a relative tuning method on the fretboard.

To use the fretboard method, start by pressing down the 6th string on the 5th fret with your 3rd finger. Then play both the open 5th string and the fretted 6th string simultaneously, and tune the 5th string until the two sounds match. Continue using this method to tune the other strings (see illustrations below).

This method might take some time to master as you develop your ear to recognize when the guitar is in tune or not. Use one of the other methods above as a reference to help train your ears.

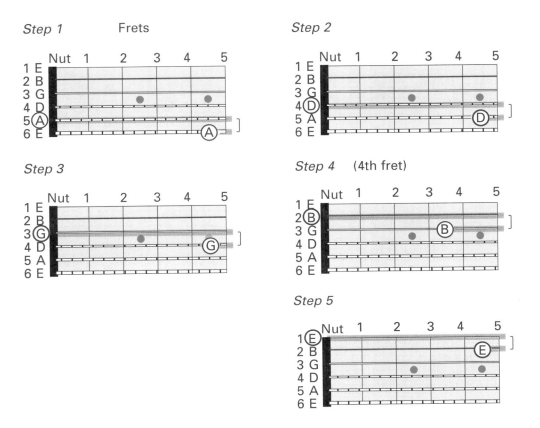

Drop Tuning

Some guitarists tune their instrument lower in pitch. An example of this is tuning the 6th string down to "Eb" and then tuning the rest of the strings down (using method no. 6) to adjust to this. Jimi occasionally used this method to transpose his songs down and make it easier on his voice to sing. This method of tuning is common in "grunge" music and has been made popular by artists such as Stevie Ray Vaughan and Eddie VanHalen, but it is not advised for a beginning guitarist. It should only be used as you progress in your ear training skills.

Accidental

The name of a pitch that has been raised, sharp (#), or lowered, flat (♭), by one half-step. A sharp or flat is restored to its original state using a natural sign (♮).

PITCH, NOTES AND OTHER MUSICAL TERMS

Pitch

The precise designation for a note at a specific frequency.

Note

The written symbol used to represent the pitch and duration of a certain sound.

Ascending (up in pitch) ———————————▶

Refers to the modulation of a pitch to a higher frequency.

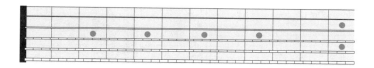

Decending (down in pitch) ◀———————————

Refers to the modulation of a pitch to a lower frequency.

Interval

The distance between two notes, measured either by whole-steps, half-steps, or a combination of both.

Here is the difference between ASCENDING a HALF-STEP and a WHOLE-STEP INTERVAL.

Half-Step

(Notice it is the fret next to the original.)

Ⓐ A# B C C# D D# E F F# G G# A

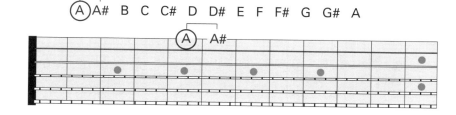

Whole-Step

(Notice you skip a fret.)

Ⓐ A# B C C# D D# E F F# G G# A

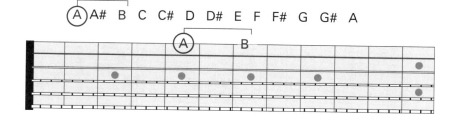

THE GUITAR NECK, KEYBOARD, AND CHROMATIC SCALE

In this section of the book, I would like to attempt to demystify the guitar neck for you. Try not to look at the guitar neck as just a mass of separate notes, but more as a specific pattern of notes climbing each string.

The guitar neck is divided into 6 CHROMATIC SCALES.

The chromatic scale is one of the easiest scales to learn—to reach the next note of the scale you simply move up one fret (half-step).

Here is the order of notes in a chromatic scale—this series of twelve half-steps covers a complete OCTAVE.

A A# B C C# D D# E F F# G G# A

This series of musical pitches is best shown on the keyboard. Notice that this scale includes ACCIDENTALS (# [sharp], ♭ [flat]), and that the B, C, E, and F are not separated by accidentals, due to the structured formula that modern Western/European music is based on.

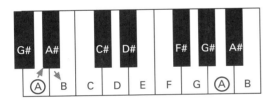

This is an example of both an "A" CHROMATIC SCALE and an OCTAVE on the 5th string of the guitar neck. See how the notes on the guitar neck correlate with the notes on the keyboard above.

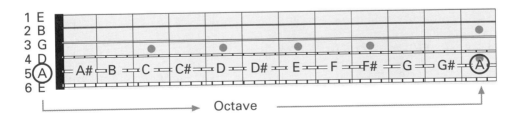

SCALE

(La., *scala,* meaning "ladder"): A sequence of notes, ascending or descending, creating a system of music. These sequences vary, using a combination of half-steps (semitones) or whole-steps (tones).

CHROMATIC SCALE

A series of musical pitches used in Western-European music, ascending or descending through a succession of half-steps (semitones).

OCTAVE

The distance between two pitches of the same name and tone, one being either half (lower) or double (higher) the frequency of the original pitch.

Guitar Neck & Chromatic Scales *(continued)*

KEY

A system of notes specifically related to each other based on a particular note, establishing the tonality of a piece of music.

TRANSPOSING

The process of changing from one series of notes to another.

Manipulating musical scales will help to enhance your understanding of their mechanics.

We will learn how to convert the KEY of the "A" Chromatic scale to the KEY of the "E" Chromatic scale; this conversion is called TRANSPOSING.

To transpose these scales you simply start at the "E" note of the chromatic scale instead of the "A" note (as shown below).

"A" Chromatic Scale → Ⓐ A# B C C# D D# E F F# G G# Ⓐ

"E" Chromatic Scale ⟶ Ⓔ F F# G G# A A# B C C# D D# Ⓔ

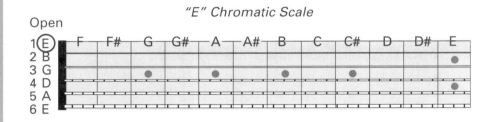

"E" Chromatic Scale

QUICK QUIZ

1. Find the name of the note on the 4th string, 7th fret.
2. Find the name of the note on the 2nd string, 8th fret.
3. Name the chromatic scale starting on the open 4th string.
4. Name the note on the 6th string, 7th fret.

Guitar Neck Reference Chart

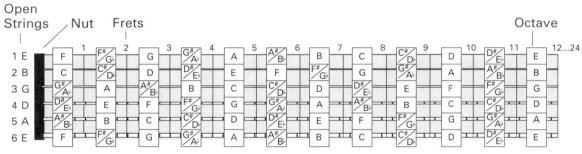

Each string has its own chromatic scale starting with the name of the open string.

With this chart as a reference, you can find any note on the fretboard.

Open String Notes/12th Fret Octaves

There is a 12th fret OCTAVE for each open guitar string. The 12th fret is usually marked with two dots.

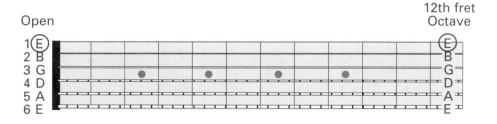

GUITAR TAB (TABLATURE)

Guitar tab is a quick and easy way to get started reading guitar music. Throughout the first half of this book we will use this method, later adding standard staff notation.

History

Guitar TABLATURE originated in the 15th century as a form of music notation for the lute. The lute is a distant relative of the guitar, having 4 to 11 strings. This form of music notation was adapted for the guitar (6 strings) and uses a method that illustrates each guitar sting, notating the fret number(s) to be played. Tablature is read from left to right, like a sentence. TAB has re-emerged as a standard for guitar players in music books, sheet music, and on the Internet.

Disadvantages

Tab lacks some key elements, such as note duration and musical expression, but used in conjunction with staff music (covered later in this book), it can be an excellent tool.

See how TAB notation correlates with the string order of the guitar grid.

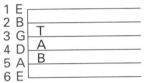
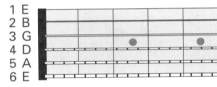

Using the tab below, play each of the open strings. Start with the 1st string "E" and end with the 6th string "E."

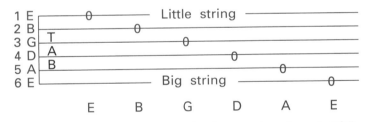

NOTE: *In TAB, numerals represent the frets to be played. "O"=open string.*

The following example illustrates the Chromatic scale (1st string) using both tab notation and the guitar grid. Use your 1st finger to climb the string one fret (half-step) at a time.

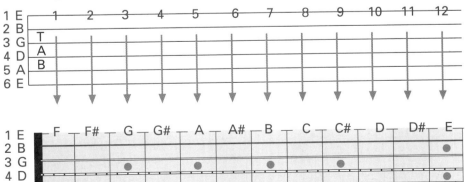

The difference between TAB and GUITAR GRIDS is:

THE GUITAR GRID

Illustrates the fingering(s) or note(s) on the frets and strings of the guitar. It shows the notes you will play in a particular piece of music, but not the sequence in which you will play them.

TABLATURE

Shows the fret number on the string to be played. Unlike the guitar grid, this method of guitar notation reads from left to right, and not only shows the notes to be played, but their sequence.

RHYTHM, TEMPO, AND BEATS

Learning HOW to play notes is just as important as knowing what notes to play. RHYTHM is the fundamental part of music, establishing its relationship to time using TEMPO and BEATS. Later in this book you will learn the music notation associated with these beats.

Musicians describe a piece of music that is played with rhythm, expression, and dynamics as being in a "GROOVE." Most musicians will agree that it is this euphoric groove that creates the bond between musician and audience.

Foot Tapping

Rhythmic structure is described in UP and/or DOWN BEATS. Notes are played in relation to these beats that can be counted by tapping your foot up and down.

You can break each beat into two parts. The DOWN BEAT (when your foot is DOWN), counted with "ONE", "TWO", "THREE", "FOUR", and the UP BEAT (when your foot is UP), counted with "AND". Beats are counted in groups of four as shown below.

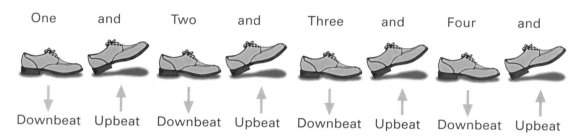

| One | and | Two | and | Three | and | Four | and |

| Downbeat | Upbeat | Downbeat | Upbeat | Downbeat | Upbeat | Downbeat | Upbeat |

Later in this book, we will describe how FOOT TAPPING correlates with WHOLE and HALF NOTES.

Tools for Developing Timing

Metronome—A simple device that produces clicks on every beat. Adjustments can be made to vary the TEMPO or the speed. This instrument is designed to help the user develop a sense of timing.

Drum Machine—This electronic instrument is designed to imitate the drums. It produces a variety of sounds, tempos, and patterns in which to practice. You can simulate playing with a band and develop your timing.

CD's and Tapes—Once you learn a song, one of the best ways to practice your rhythm, speed, and technique is to actually play along with a CD/tape. Try to choose songs that match your playing ability.

You should be aware that some recordings employ multiple tracks of the same instrument. For now, you should focus on learning one track.

Playing with Other Musicians—This can be one of the most exciting aspects of playing an instrument. Playing with others can challenge all of your new skills: tuning, rhythm, timing, and technique. Depending on the experience of the other players, be prepared to make adjustments for fluctuating talents. Be aware of this and use this time as an overall learning experience. It is helpful if everybody practices the songs before you get together.

THE MAJOR SCALE

STEP ONE: The Major Pattern

The major scale is based on a specific PATTERN, and this pattern is essential to understanding the basics of music. The major scale can start with any note within a chromatic scale; this note establishes the KEY of the scale. The KEY NOTE (root note) is followed by a specific order of HALF and WHOLE-STEPS as follows:

w=whole-step (skip a whole fret)

h=half-step (go to next fret)

1	w	2	w	3	h	4	w	5	w	6	w	7	h	8
1st note		2nd note		3rd note		4th note		5th note		6th note		7th note		octave

STEP TWO: The Major Pattern on the 1st "E" String

The easiest string to learn this pattern on is the 1st string (E). This pattern is illustrated below, both on the guitar grid and in tab. Start by playing the first note open (E), then climbing the frets with your 1st finger to start with. Later in this book you will develop skills using your other fingers. For now concentrate on using and memorizing the positions of this scale on your guitar neck.

The major scale can be associated with DO, RE, MI, FA, SOL, LA, TI, DO.

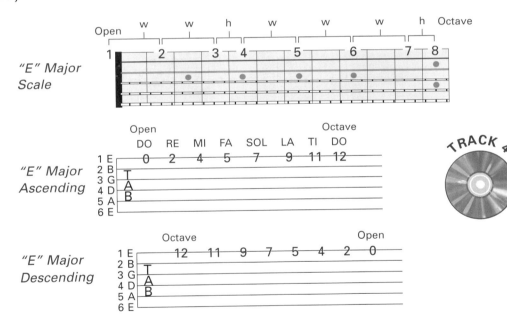

"E" Major Scale

"E" Major Ascending

"E" Major Descending

TRACK 4

STEP THREE: The Notes of the "E" Major Scale

Here are the actual notes of the "E" Major scale that you just played:

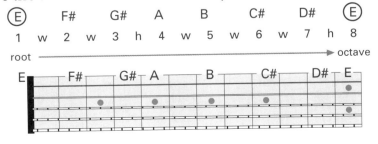

The MAJOR (DIATONIC) SCALE is one of the fundamental scales used in Western music. This 7 NOTE scale is described as having a "happy" or "pleasant" tone, compared to the CHROMATIC SCALE (page 11,12) which retains a quality of tension. The major scale, derived from an early Greek system of music, can also be referred to as the IONIAN MODE. Melodies, chords, and solos are often comprised of the notes from this scale.

TIP

Remember the dot position markers are on the odd (3, 5, 7, 9) frets and the octave on the 12th. This can be an important reference for you to track where you are as you play up and down the guitar neck.

"E" MAJOR SCALE MELODIES

Now let's use notes from the "E" Major scale to play a familiar melody that was performed by Jimi Hendrix. We have highlighted the notes that you will be playing and provided the order to be played in tab.

Notes to be played (not in sequence):

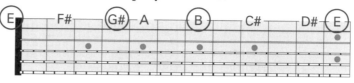

EXERCISE 1: Introduction to STAR SPANGLED BANNER

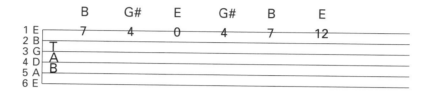

The full version of this song will be taught later in this book. The scales that you will be learning were used to compose many of your favorite Jimi Hendrix songs. Try listening for them!

EXERCISE 2: Jumping Octave on the "E" String

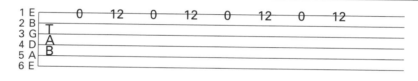

EXERCISE 3: Major (3 Note Set) Run

This exercise is a challenge to your new skills. Remember to take your time on each line and to enjoy the learning process. Start slow and gradually build up your speed. These exercises have a building effect on all of your other guitar skills. Below each tab notation, I will supply a suggested fingering number. You might find this fingering a little difficult at first. If you do, practice this exercise with one finger; this still allows you to experience this run of notes.

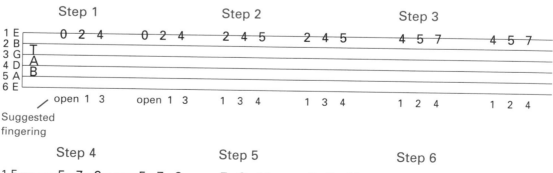

Suggested fingering

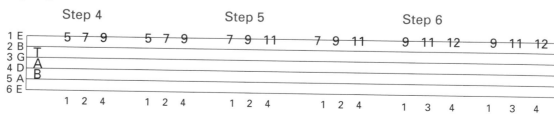

More exercises available on the Internet at www.jimi-hendrix.com.

Once you have learned a scale, you can use the notes to play a MELODY. A melody is an arrangement of single notes used for musical expression; usually this is the portion of a song that you remember, the part that "gets stuck in your head."

PRACTICE HABITS

1. Try to break a long piece of music into sections.

2. Practice a section of music at least 3 or 4 times (or more) through.

3. Practice very slowly at first, then increase the speed.

4. Try to memorize the section.

5. Hum to yourself the notes you are practicing.

TRANSPOSING MAJOR SCALES

Remember the concept of TRANSPOSING the Chromatic scale shown earlier on page 12? You can also use this method to transpose the Major scale. The main element in transposing a Major scale to a different key is the consistent pattern of the scale's structure, meaning that the whole and half-step pattern remains the same.

Below, we will demonstrate transposing the "E" Major Scale (1st string) to the "A" Major scale (5th string). Notice how both scales have the same whole and half-step pattern. Various songs are written in different keys, so it is helpful to understand the concept of transposing.

"E" Major Scale (shown earlier)

Whole and half-step pattern:

Pattern shown on guitar grid:

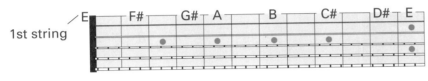

Notes in TAB:

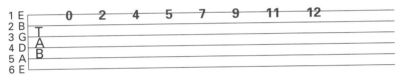

"A" Major Scale

Whjole and half-step pattern:

Pattern shown on guitar grid:

Notes in TAB:

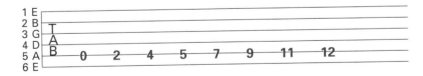

Here are the major scales for each of the open strings. (Notice that the patterns are all the same.)

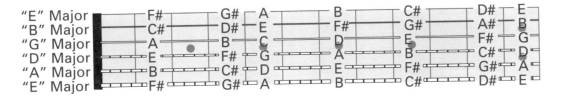

THIRD STONE FROM THE SUN— "A" MAJOR SCALE

QUICK START

In this section you will use the "A" Major scale to create the classic solo from the Hendrix instrumental *Third Stone From the Sun*. This is an excellent exercise for practicing your new skills.

5th string — A — B — C# — D — E — F# — G# — A

Learning How to Slide

In this section of the solo you will need to learn how to SLIDE between notes. In order to slide a note on a single string, first play the note and, while main-taining constant pressure on the string, drag your finger to the next note illus-trated.

In TAB a slide is represented by an angled line such as this:

PART ONE

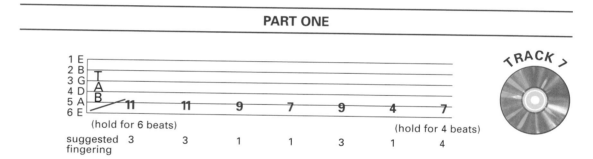

TRACK 7

(hold for 6 beats)   (hold for 4 beats)

suggested fingering   3   3   1   1   3   1   4

PART TWO

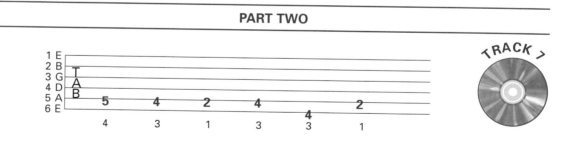

TRACK 7

4   3   1   3   3   1

PART THREE

Jam with Jimi (resampled)! Note: Jimi's guitar is droptuned to "E♭".

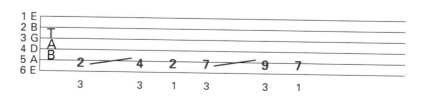

TRACK 7

3   3   1   3   3   1

18

DRONE STRINGS

A BITONAL (or DRONE) string can be used as an effect to enhance the single string scales that you have just learned. This sound is reminiscent of the East Indian instrument, the SITAR. To achieve this effect, you will play the scale in the same manner as you learned earlier, but you will also play the string just above it at the same time. This gives the DRONING effect that Jimi incorporated into his music.

Let's play the "A" Major scale on the 5th string (page 17), but this time pick both the 5th and the 6th strings at the same time. Notice the drone effect that we have just described.

"A" Major Scale: A w B w C# h D w E w F# w G# h A

Pattern shown on guitar grid:

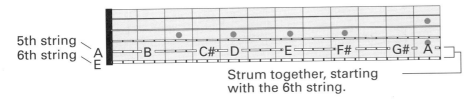

TRACK 9

Notes in TAB:

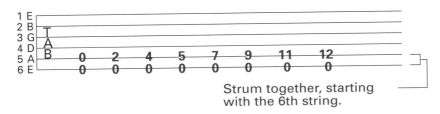

THIRD STONE FROM THE SUN—Using Drone String Exercise

In this section you will repeat the melody that you learned earlier, but this time you will include the "E" DRONE string. Notice how adding this extra string creates a fuller sound. Be sure not to mute the 6th "E" string as this could cancel the effect you want to create in this exercise.

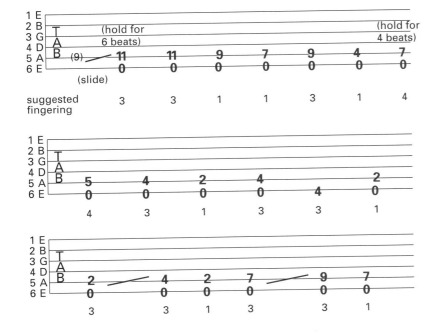

TRACK 9

Note: Jimi actually plays this melody line in octaves.

Memorizing

Try memorizing small sections of music first instead of the entire song or musical piece. This allows you to concentrate and absorb the specific sections, and to allow you to perform the song to the best of your ability. Only after you feel confident with these smaller sections should you focus on practicing the entire song or musical piece.

THE MINOR SCALE (MODE)

The MINOR (NATURAL) scale is a fundamental scale used heavily in rock and blues music. This 7-note scale is described as having a "sad" or "somber" tone, compared to the major scale which has more of a "happy" tone. You can also describe their differences as MODES, or the mood of their sound. The Minor scale, like the Major scale, was derived from an early Greek system of music, and can also be referred to as the AEOLIAN MODE. In this Greek system of music both the Major (IONIAN) and the Minor (AEOLIAN) scale can consist of the same notes, only arranged in a different order. In this relationship the scales are said to be RELATIVE.

Example: "C" Ionian—C, D, E, F, G, A, B, C

"A" Aeolian —A, B, C, D, E, F, G, A

There is a simple method of transforming a Major scale into a Minor scale using a parallel conversion. To simplify this concept we will use the 1st string (E) to demonstrate the difference between the "E" Major and the "E" Minor scales.

Converting an "E" Major Scale into "E" Minor Scale

To convert the Major scale to the Minor scale simply move the 3rd, 6th, and 7th notes down a half-step as illustrated below. (You can also refer to this as FLATTING ($\flat$) the 3rd, 6th, and 7th.)

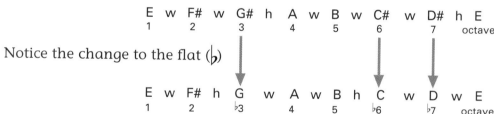

"E" Major Scale

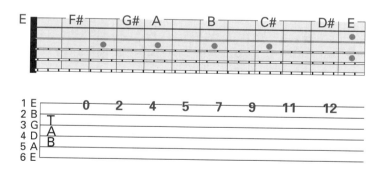

"E" Minor Scale

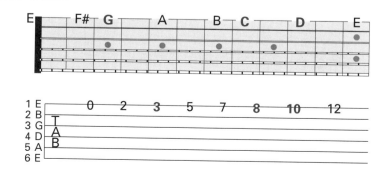

USING THE "E" MINOR SCALE— HIGHWAY CHILE, GUITAR INTRO

QUICK START

The introduction of *Highway Chile* can be played within the notes of the "E" Minor scale. Due to your skill level, this song has been transposed down one half-step from the original recording. Here are the notes that you will use in the "E" Minor scale.

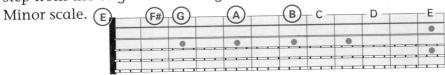

HIGHWAY CHILE

Part One

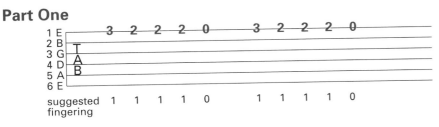

TRACK 11

Part Two

Jimi plays a BASS note on the guitar after each phrase. This lower note is played at the same time as the drums and bass to add a punchy effect to the song. Try playing the same section you learned earlier, but this time using these extra notes.

Part One

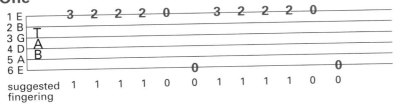

TRACK 11

Part Two

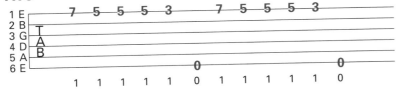

TRACK 11

JAM WITH JIMI

TRACK 12

THEORY

Two-String Unison Bend

Jimi also uses an advanced guitar technique in this introduction that utilizes the 1st and 2nd strings, by bending up the 2nd string to match the note on the 1st string. Playing with your index finger on the 3rd fret of the 1st string, BEND with your 3rd finger on the 6th fret of the 2nd string, which gives a fuller sound to the introduction. This technique is very difficult and should be used later as your skills advance.

"G" Unison Bend

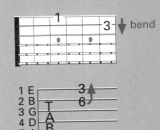

21

PICKING

Picking is an important function of playing the guitar. Your picking hand is a driving element for the rhythm of your instrument. It has the function of selecting the notes, expression and volume of your music. As you practice the exercises in the following pages, make sure you maintain contact with your guitar by either holding your lower palm against the bridge or by holding your little finger against the guitar body just below the strings (see page 6).

Exercise 1

Start with your 6th string (big E) and practice picking 8 times without looking at the string. Practice all three methods shown below.

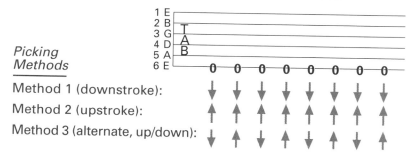

Picking Methods

Method 1 (downstroke):

Method 2 (upstroke):

Method 3 (alternate, up/down):

Exercise 2

Practice from the 6th string on up to the 1st using the picking methods above.

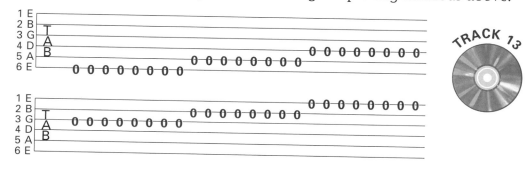

TRACK 13

Exercise 3

Practice from the 1st string on up to the 6th using the picking methods above.

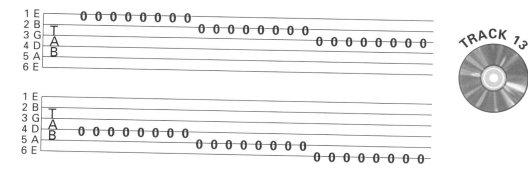

TRACK 13

Exercise 4

Now try playing up and down the strings one at a time.

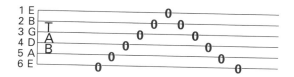

TRACK 13

NOTE

For most people, picking UP is more difficult than picking DOWN. Try to compensate for this by spending extra time on developing your UP stroke. ALTERNATE picking is what will eventually allow you to generate the most speed; but if you are not even on the strokes (up and down) this could effect how your picking flows. Imagine drawing a circle on the guitar string, catching the string with the angled sidetip of the pick on the up and down stroke of the circle. Use your wrist as a pivot of the motion you're picking, not your whole arm. Keep your arm and wrist relaxed!

BUGLE TAPS

Jimi spent some time in the US Army, so I assume that these melodies rang through his head first thing in the morning (grin). The following melodies are common military bugle taps that can be played on all open strings and are a great picking exercise for you to practice.

Tap One

You might recognize this melody from the baseball games. Be aware of the notes on the 2nd string, 3rd fret.

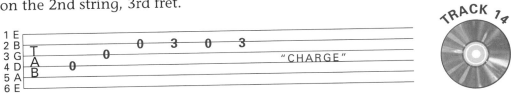

Tap Two

This next melody is used in military funerals. This tap uses one fretted note on string 2.

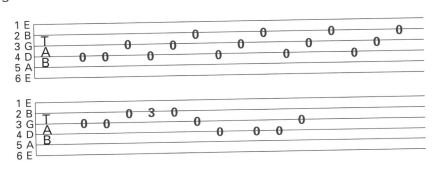

Tap Three

This is a common wake-up call used in the military. On this melody you might need to watch your picking hand at first. You should practice enough so that you no longer need to.

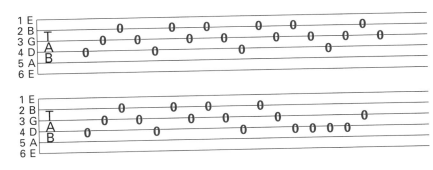

POWER CHORDS (5 CHORDS)

THEORY

A key element and coloration of music is the structure of CHORDS. A chord is defined as being three or more different notes that are played simultaneously. In this section of the book we'll explore how chords are built, proper fingering, and how chords are used in music.

A common chord used in modern music is the MAJOR CHORD. This chord is based upon specific notes of the MAJOR SCALE. We'll start with the "A" Major scale (5th string) since you've already learned this scale earlier on page 17.

The formula of the "A" Major chord is derived from the 1st, 3rd, and 5th notes of the "A" Major scale.

Root Notes

The first note of a scale in reference to building a chord is called the ROOT note of the chord.

Major Chord Formula: root (1), 3, 5

"A" Major Scale:	A root	B 2	C# 3	D 4	E 5	F# 6	G# 7	A octave
"A" Major Chord:	A		C#		E			

Now that you understand how Major chords are built, we'll go to the next step and use this formula to create a POWER CHORD (otherwise known as a 5 CHORD). Later in this book (pages 46, 47) we'll concentrate on the Major chords, but it is important when learning Jimi's music to understand the concept of chords and to start out with Power Chords.

POWER OR 5 CHORDS

The more traditional schools of music regard the 5 Chord as an "interval" (page 10) rather than a "chord." Remember that chords are defined as three or more notes played simultaneously (root, 3, 5, etc.). With a 5 Chord, only two notes (root, 5) are played. Regardless of whether or not it is an "official" chord, the 5 Chord is used consistently by most musicians in both rock and blues. The root and 5th (also called the PERFECT FIFTH because of its tonal relationship to the ROOT NOTE) of a scale, when played simultaneously, produce an "audio image" of sounding the same, but harmonically different. This "image" gives the chord a powerful sound, resulting in the nickname, the Power Chord.

Major Chord Formula: root (1), 3, 5

"A" Major Scale:	A root	B 2	C# 3	D 4	E 5	F# 6	G# 7	A octave
"A" 5 Power Chord:	A				E			

PRACTICE TIP

Keeping the Beat

Think of your picking hand as a rhythm instrument, much like the drums. You can experiment by strumming your guitar string in various rhythmic patterns. With this hand you can develop a groove which is one key element of music.

Pick Without Looking

Practice picking without looking at your picking hand; you can then concentrate on your guitar neck and increase your speed. Try practicing while watching television; you will be distracted from looking at your hand and will develop your muscle memory.

Here is the "A" Major Scale on the 5th string. In order to play the root and the fifth simultaneously, we will have to find where this fifth note is played on the 4th string. The scale in Step 1 is the scale we learned on pages 17 and 24.

STEP ONE: "A" Major Scale
(finding the unison FIFTH note on the 4th string)

Pattern shown on guitar grid:

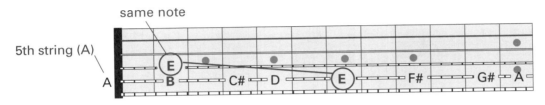

Notes in TAB:

STEP TWO: "A" Major Scale

Below is an illustration of how to play the "A" Major scale using the same notes as in Step One, but continuing onto the 3rd and 4th strings rather than climbing the scale on only the 5th string.

Pattern shown on guitar grid:

Notes in TAB:

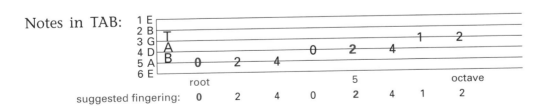

PRACTICE TIP

Play with Your Eyes Closed

Once you have mastered a section of music, try practicing the part without looking at your hands, or better yet, with your eyes closed. You will not be tempted to rely on your vision, and you can test the motor skills that you have developed. Although this may not be practical for all of the parts that you will play, it can be an excellent learning tool.

25

POWER CHORDS *(continued)*

OPEN "A" (5) POWER CHORDS

Here is how you can play "A" (5) Power Chords. Below are three different ways to show the "A" (5) Power Chord. You can also incorporate the OCTAVE of the scale into the Power Chord. This extra note doesn't change the name of the chord because it's identical to the ROOT, only higher. Adding the octave produces a fuller sound.

"A" 5 Power Chords:

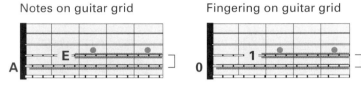

"A" 5 Power Chords (with octave)

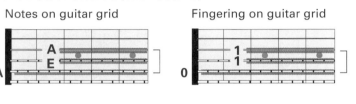

Fretted "A" (5) Power Chords

An interesting aspect about the structure of the guitar versus other instruments (piano, brass, woodwinds, etc.) is that you can find the identical notes, scales, and chords duplicated throughout the guitar neck. Below I demonstrate how to find the identical "A" Major scale and the "A" (5) Power Chord on other strings. In this illustration we are not TRANSPOSING but simply finding the identical scale and chords on the guitar neck.

Pattern shown on guitar grid:

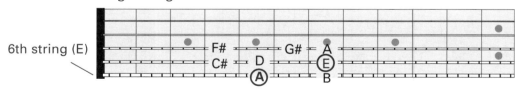

Notes in TAB:

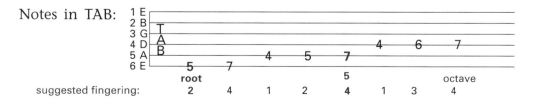

Compare the above scale to the "A" Major scale on the previous page.

Here is the "A" (5) Power Chord starting on the 6th string, 5th fret. Notice that you use your 1st finger on the 6th string, 5th fret and your 3rd finger on the 5th string, 7th fret.

TRACK 16

"A" 5 Power Chords:

Notes on guitar grid

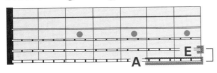

Fingering on guitar grid

Shown in TAB

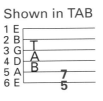

Here is the "A" (5) Power Chord with the octave (A) added. Play this chord the same as the illustration above, but also add your 4th finger on the 4th string, 7th fret.

TRACK 16

"A" 5 Power Chords (with octave)

Notes on guitar grid

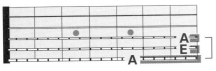

Fingering on guitar grid

Shown in TAB

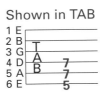

NOTE: These chords can be challenging for most people at first. Eventually with practice you will master them and be able to play a great number of popular songs!

OPEN POWER CHORDS—TRANSPOSED

The cool thing about Power Chords is that once you've learned the fingerings of these chords (both versions: open and up the frets), they can simply be moved in various neck positions, either by transposing to a different KEY, or by playing within the scale. I know that keeping track of all of the notes can be confusing and tricky. Try to think of it as simply moving the same fingering pattern up and down the neck and onto different strings. Remember to be aware of what ROOT notes you are playing with each Power Chord, as this will allow you to find your chord quickly. First we will go through the concept of transposing a chord.

POWER CHORDS *(continued)*

TRANSPOSED (continued)

Here again is the "A" Major scale and the Open "A" (5) Power Chord:

PRACTICE TIP

Walk the Walk
Talk the Talk

Observe other guitar players. There is so much you can learn by watching concerts, club bands, TV, videos, friends, etc., etc., etc. Local music stores are a great place to get information. Start a collection of music books and guitar magazines as these resources are rich in content. Be like a sponge and absorb what you can! Also, try to find a good, reputable teacher; this important step can catapult your learning experience!

"A" Major Scale and the Open "A" (5) Power Chord

Pattern shown on guitar grid:

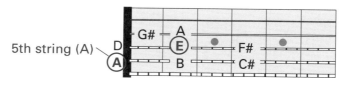

TRACK 17

5th string (A)

"A" (5) Power Chord

Notes in TAB:

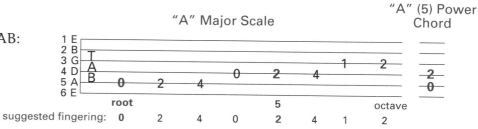

"A" Major Scale

suggested fingering: 0   2   4   0   2   4   1   2

Here below is the same pattern moved to the key of "E" (6th string). Notice that the patterns are exactly the same, only they start with the "E" (which then becomes the ROOT NOTE).

"E" Major Scale and the Open "E" (5) Power Chord

Pattern shown on guitar grid:

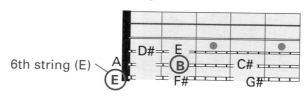

TRACK 17

6th string (E)

"E" (5) Power Chord

Notes in TAB:

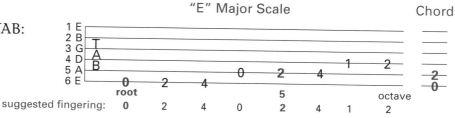

"E" Major Scale

suggested fingering: 0   2   4   0   2   4   1   2

POWER CHORDS—USED WITHIN THE SCALE (RELATIVE)

Chords can also be moved within the framework of a scale. Below is a breakdown of these steps to illustrate their construction. These chords can also be termed as RELATIVE, due to their relationship to each other.

"A" Major Scale (extended on the 6th string)

Pattern shown on extended guitar grid:

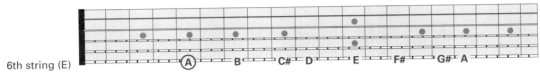

Notes in TAB:

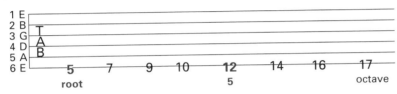

Now extend the "A" Major scale on the 5th string into the next octave of the scale. These two scales consist of the same notes, but are on different strings and frets.

"A" Major Scale (6th string with 5th string extended into next octave)

Pattern shown on extended guitar grid:

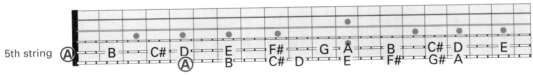

Well, I'll bet you're confused at this point. But if we diagram the relationship of the two "A" Major scales, and show the Power Chord for each note in the KEY, it hopefully becomes clearer. Now try to play each Power Chord, following the TAB notation on the following page.

ATTENTION

At first, this section may be difficult to understand or play on the acoustic guitar. Try your best to get an understanding of the concept and occasionally review this section until you understand.

PRACTICE TIP

Remember, Even Jimi Wasn't Always a Great Player!

All great players at some point in their lives were learning, just like you! Playing music can be an endless, rewarding experience. There are many styles and techniques, so take it day by day and explore the possibilities.

QUICK START

USED WITHIN THE SCALE (continued)

Here we go!

Power Chords related within the "A" Major Scale (6th string)

TRACK 18

Pattern shown on extended guitar grid:

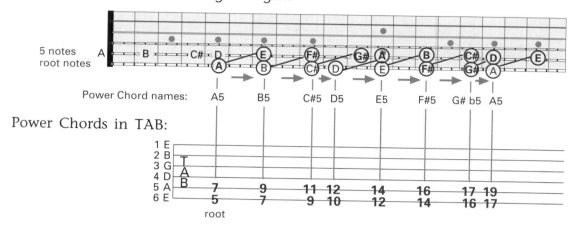

Power Chords in TAB:

5 Chord Graph:

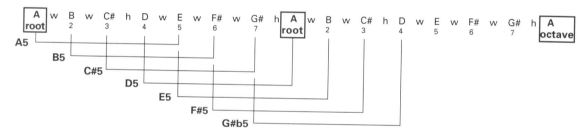

The chords we just learned are also on the 5th string.

Power Chords related within the "A" Major Scale (5th string)

TRACK 18

Pattern shown on extended guitar grid:

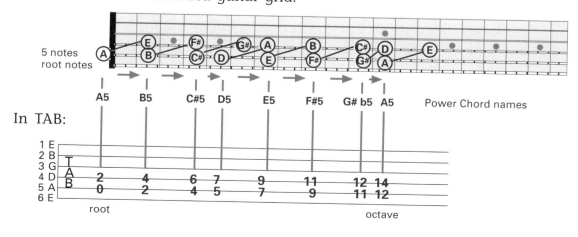

In TAB:

The guitar neck is structured so that the ROOT note of the POWER CHORD is on the lower string (6th) and the 5th note of the chord is on the string (5th) just above it and two frets away. Remember, you use your 1st and 3rd fingers to play this chord. These chords can be found on the other strings as well. The 7th note (G#) is the only chord that doesn't work out to be a perfect 5th note; this chord is called a G#b5 interval.

ROCK PROGRESSIONS— 5 POWER CHORDS

Common Rock Progressions

All songs are based on a PROGRESSION in one way or another. A progression is a group of notes or chords that are related within a scale ("A" Major in this case) and played in various sequences to create music.

Root, 4, 5

The most common rock progression is built on the root, 4th, and 5th notes of the scale. This progression evolved from early BLUES PROGRESSIONS. Below is an illustration of the "A" Major scale rock progression.

| A root | w | B 2 | w | C# 3 | h | D 4 | w | E 5 | w | F# 6 | w | G# 7 | h | A octave |

A (root), D (4), and E (5) are the notes and chords used in WILD THING. Below I've illustrated these notes of the progression on the 6th string of the guitar grid.

"A" Major: root, 4, 5 notes

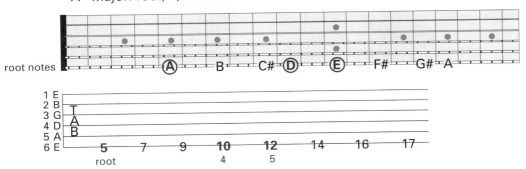

Root, 4, 5 Power Chords Related within the "A" Major Scale (6th string)

Below are the power chords that are based on the root (A5), 4 (D5), and 5 (E5) illustrated on the 6th string of the guitar grid.

| A root | w | B 2 | w | C# 3 | h | D 4 | w | E 5 | w | F# 6 | w | G# 7 | h | A octave |

Pattern shown on extended guitar grid:

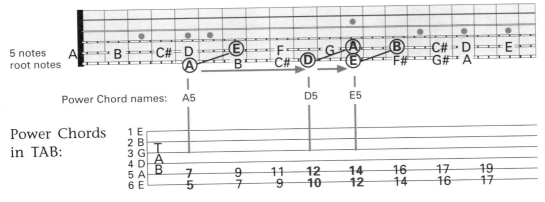

WILD THING

Using Power Chords and the Root, 4, 5 Progression

Jimi's famous for playing *Wild Thing* at Monterey and burning his guitar on stage while the music droned on. Well, we're not going to practice techniques in burning the guitar just yet—that lesson will be in book three (just kidding!)—but we will explore *Wild Thing* using the theory that we've just covered. You will learn different ways of playing this song in order to apply and practice the information you have learned so far. So, if you're ready...let's rock!

VERSION 1

Note: This version may be difficult on the acoustic guitar.

In this version of *Wild Thing* we will use the "A" Major Root, 4, 5 Progression based on the 6th string (see previous page).

EXERCISE 1—Root Notes

Here is the root note (bass) version of the chorus and verse to *Wild Thing*.

EXERCISE 2—Power Chords

Here is the Power Chord version of the chorus and verse to *Wild Thing*.

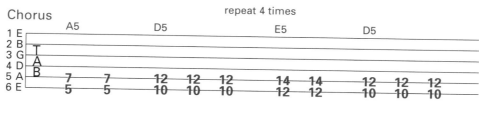

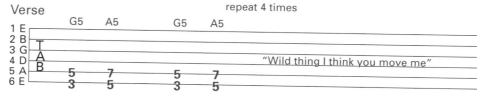

VERSION 2—Root, 4, 5, "L" Shape Pattern

Remember what we learned on page 29—that the same notes that are on the 6th string can be found on the 5th string as well? In this version of *Wild Thing*, we will use this knowledge to move the Power Chords from version 1. Illustrated below is the "A" Major Scale and related root, 4, 5 Power Chords.

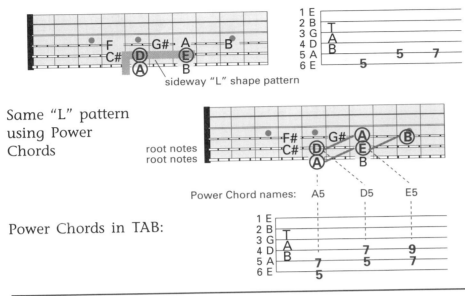

sideway "L" shape pattern

Same "L" pattern using Power Chords

root notes
root notes

Power Chord names: A5   D5   E5

Power Chords in TAB:

Notice that the pattern of the Root, 4, 5 makes an "L" shape on the guitar neck. Remember this pattern whenever you're using the Root, 4, 5 on two strings.

EXERCISE 1—Root Notes

Here is the root note (bass) version of the chorus and verse to *Wild Thing*.

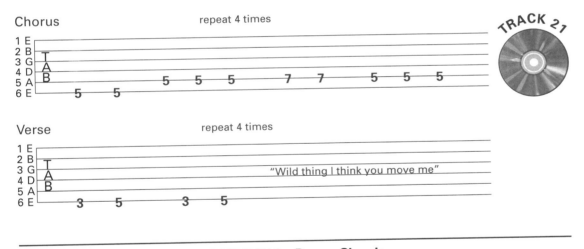

Chorus   repeat 4 times   TRACK 21

Verse   repeat 4 times

"Wild thing I think you move me"

EXERCISE 2—Power Chords

Here is the Power Chord version of the chorus and verse to *Wild Thing*.

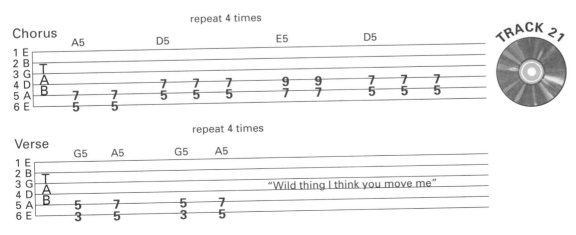

Chorus   repeat 4 times   TRACK 21
A5   D5   E5   D5

Verse   repeat 4 times
G5   A5   G5   A5

"Wild thing I think you move me"

33

WILD THING (continued)

VERSION 3—Open Power Chords

Wild Thing can also be played with open power chords. You do have one adjustment with these chords, however. The "E" (5) Power Chord, also the 5th note of this progression, is played an octave lower.

This scale has been extended with lower notes.

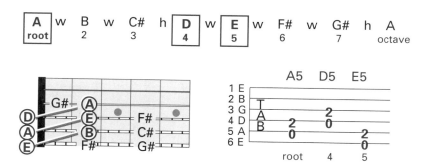

REMEMBER

The three versions of *Wild Thing* were not given to you simply to impress your friends with how many places on the neck of the guitar you can play the same song (of course, your friends may be easily impressed). These versions were designed to exercise the skills that you will need in order to perform other songs, as well as help you learn the fretboard.

TIP

Listen for this progression in songs such as *Louie Louie*, and other rock and blues tunes.

EXERCISE 1—Root Notes

Here is the Root Note (bass) version of the chorus and verse to *Wild Thing*.

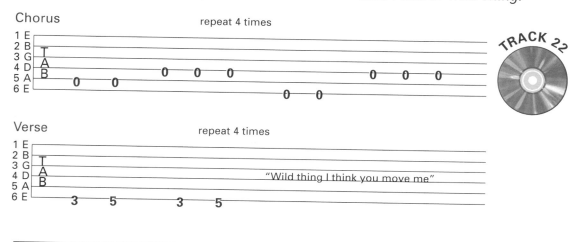

EXERCISE 2—Power Chords

Here is the Power Chord version of the chorus and verse to *Wild Thing*.

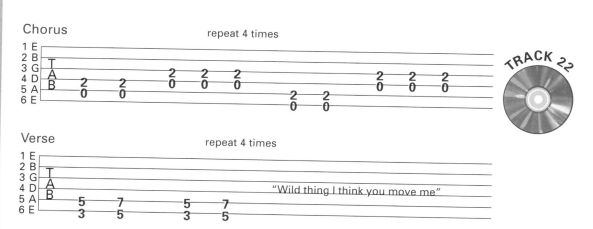

SONG STRUCTURES

Songs are structured using several common elements. Here is a list of the definitions with which you will become more familiar:

Introduction (Intro): A group of chords or notes that sets the mood of the song. It may be part of the main body of the song or a separate musical piece.

Verse: The main body of the song containing the story line or subject; the verse usually repeats throughout the song.

Chorus: The part of the song that repeats the main HOOK or theme of the song.

Bridge: Usually the middle of the song that is different from the verse and chorus. It usually comes immediately before the SOLO.

Solo: Generally in the middle section of the song where the guitar stands out as the lead instrument. The solo was the highlight of Jimi's songs; he seemed to take the guitar to a different dimension.

Common Terms

Hook: A short, catchy musical or lyrical phrase. Usually the part of the song that everyone knows.

Riff: A short musical phrase that is repeated throughout a piece of music.

Lick: Also a short musical phrase, however it is generally not repeated. Generally a lick is thought of as a part of the solo.

Run: A quick climb or descent through a scale.

Here is the common formula for one of Jimi's songs:

Intro
Verse
Chorus
Verse
Chorus
Bridge
Solo (comprised of Licks, Riffs, Hooks, Runs and a little bit of God)
Verse
Chorus
End

FOXEY LADY

Foxey Lady was the one song that Jimi was totally satisfied with the way it was written. This is an excellent song for learning and understanding basic techniques of the guitar and song structure. In the breakdown of this song you will learn the following:

1. The key of "E."

2. Playing two strings at the same time.

3. Using the picking technique to play various strings.

4. The "E" Minor Blues scale.

5. Playing 5 (Power) Chords.

6. Guitar techniques such as:

   Slides

   Vibrato

   Feedback

7. How to play *Foxey Lady!*

Foxey Lady is a classic for all of us who love Jimi's music. When played in F# (recorded version), this song can be difficult for a beginner. Instead of putting your fingers through a series of acrobatic hoops, I transposed *Foxey Lady* down a whole step to "E" so you can perform this song with ease (although nothing of Jimi's is easy). In the recording, Jimi overdubs other guitar tracks to give the song a fuller sound. In this transcript, you will be learning some of these main RIFFS.

VERSE—Riff 1 (Simplified)

Step 1

Hold your 3rd finger down on the 1st and 2nd string on the 3rd fret as shown in the illustration to the right.

Test the two notes by playing one string at a time to make sure they sound right (not muted), then strum both 1st and 2nd strings at the same time (they should both ring together).

Be sure you hold both strings down tight.

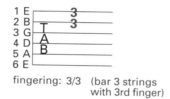

fingering: 3/3   (bar 3 strings with 3rd finger)

TRACK 23

Step 2

Now try the main line of *Foxey Lady*. Keeping your position as illustrated above, pick with your right hand and first play the open 6th string (2 times) and then strum the 1st and 2nd string at the same time (play it 3 times).

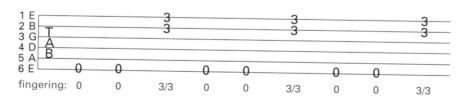

fingering: 0   0   3/3   0   0   3/3   0   0   3/3

TRACK 23

Step 3

There are two extra notes added to this first phrase that you play on the 3rd and 5th frets of your 6th string using your 2nd finger (or thumb). This is the basic version riff of the verse.

TRACK 23

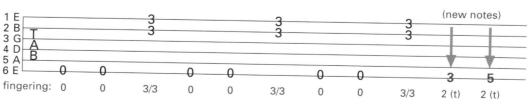

fingering: 0   0   3/3   0   0   3/3   0   0   3/3   2 (t)   2 (t)

Step 1

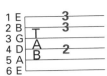

Hold your 3rd finger down on the 1st and 2nd string on the 3rd fret as shown. Then hold your 1st finger on the 4th string, 2nd fret.

Step 2

Now start the riff as you played earlier, but this time when you come up to the 3rd note of this phrase, play the 4th string, then resume playing the rest of this riff as before.

TRACK 24

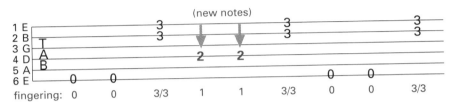

Step 3

Here is the full verse riff with the changing bass line added.

TRACK 24

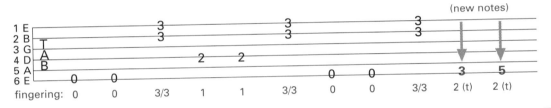

VERSE—Riff 3 (Changing Bass Line with Blues Run)

Step 1

Play Step 2 of Riff 2 (above) again.

Step 2

Add these extra notes based on the "E" Minor Blues scale. You can play these notes by sliding up your 2nd finger or using your thumb (optional).

"E" MINOR BLUES SCALE

E G A B♭ B D E

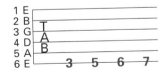

TRACK 24

Step 3

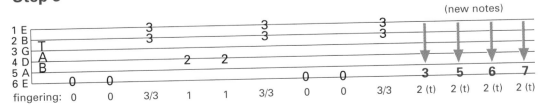

Riff 3 is basically the same as Riff 2, but this time we will add a few notes at the end of the phrase, based on "E" Minor Blues Scale which we will cover in more depth later.

FOXEY LADY *(continued)*

There are a lot of guitar tracks going on during the verse of *Foxey Lady*. Try to focus your ear on one of the following options. Start off with Option 1; when you progress, try Option 2. Be aware that there is a Bass track that is doubled by the guitar on a track. Don't let these extra tracks confuse you. Just focus on what you have learned.

Remember all of those exercises we focused on in Power Chords? Here is where you can use these skills to your advantage. The CHORUS of *Foxey Lady* consists of all OPEN POWER CHORDS (page 26). The chords we will use are the E5, D5, and A5.

PRACTICING THE VERSE TO JIMI'S RECORDING

TRACK 25

Option 1 (Easy Version)

Play this verse three times through.

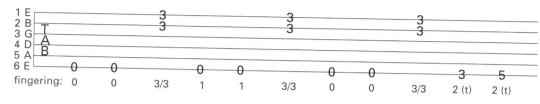

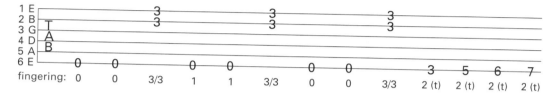

Option 2 (Challenging Version)

TRACK 25

Play this verse three times through.

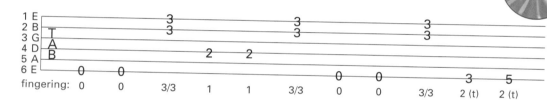

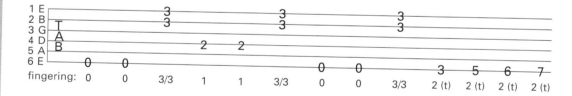

CHORUS —Power Chords (5 Chords)

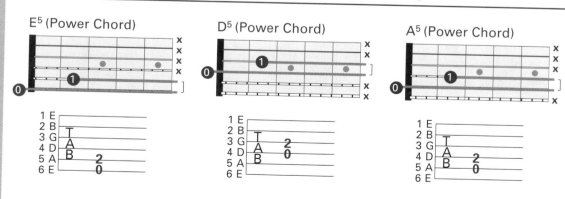

E5 (Power Chord)   D5 (Power Chord)   A5 (Power Chord)

Chorus—Part 1

Play three times through.

TRACK 26

In this section of *Foxey Lady* you will learn how to BEND the guitar string up to a higher note. To bend the string you will need to use your 3rd finger and the support of your 2nd finger, in order to have the strength to bend the string up one WHOLE step in pitch. In this case you will be bending "A" up to "B."

To test the comparison between the pitches, play the two notes without bending, and then practice bending up to the correct pitch. This technique is difficult on the acoustic guitar and guitars with heavy gauge strings.

Practice

Play the 5th fret, 1st string (A) and then 7th fret, 1st string (B).

Now play the 1st string, 5th fret (with 3rd finger as described above) and try to bend your 1st string up one whole step until you match the pitch of the "B."

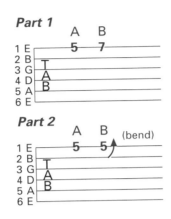

TRACK 27

Notice in the left illustration below how the 1st string is bent up with your 3rd finger. See how the 2nd finger is used for additional support. Remember not to collapse your thumb, but to use it as a support to grab the neck to help bend the string up.

Chorus—Part 2 (Lead Lick)

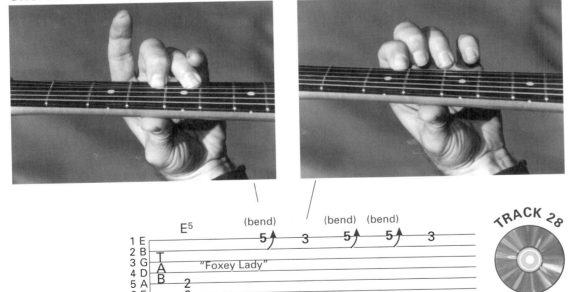

TRACK 28

Now You Can Play *Foxey Lady* Clear Through!

TRACK 29

To play the full transcript, play one of the VERSE options on the previous page (three times), followed by *part one* of the CHORUS (three times), then *part two* of the CHORUS (above). When you are finished, repeat to the beginning.

There are a few techniques that Jimi uses in the introduction to *Foxey Lady* that you can begin to practice.

Vibrato

Hold your 3rd finger (supported by your 2nd finger) on the 3rd string, 9th fret. Now bend your finger slightly to vary the pitch. Try to match the speed of Jimi (well, go as fast as you can).

Feedback

Achieved when you face your guitar to the amp with it "cranked up" (try not to bother the neighbors with this one).

Sliding

Place your finger on the guitar string and slide it up or down as fast as you can (this one may hurt a bit when you first start out).

THE BLUES

Root, 4, and 5 Progressions

Earlier in this book (page 31) we covered how the root, 4, 5 progression is taken from the Major scale. The BLUES PROGRESSION uses this same formula, but takes it a step further.

(page 31)

Step 1

Here is a single note run up the "A" Major root, 4, 5, on the 5th string.

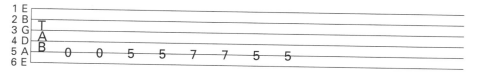

A common blues progression uses this pattern: Root (R) 4, R, 5, 4, R, 5.

Step 2

Practice this "A" Blues Progression.

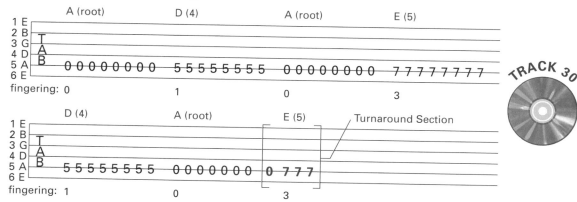

Step 3

Practice this "A" Blues Progression using the 5 (Power) Chords.

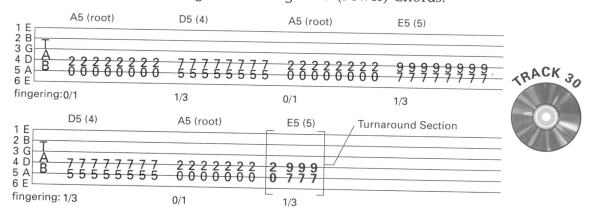

Turnarounds

The section at the end of a Blues Progression (in brackets in the progression above) that RESOLVES the phrase and/or launches it to the beginning of the progression is called a TURNAROUND. This section may consist of a few notes or chords and can vary in length.

In this section you'll see why the BLUES is considered the foundation for contemporary ROCK music. We will explore the basic BLUES formula, and various patterns of blues style and you'll be able to hear and see the heavy blues influence in Jimi's guitar riffs and songs.

Notice that in the BLUES PROGRESSION, you keep returning to the ROOT note.

Root, 4, 5 (Open 5 Chords)

Now we'll play the BLUES ROOT, 4, 5, PROGRESSION using OPEN notes and 5 (Power) Chords.

"A" Blues Progression (Notes)

A		D	A	E	D	A	E
ROOT (R)		4	R	5	4	R	5

Step 1

"A" Blues Progression using open notes:

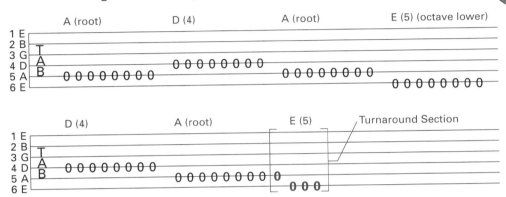

"A" Blues Progression (Notes)

A5		D5	A5	E5	D5	A5	E5
ROOT (R)		4	R	5	4	R	5

Step 2

"A" Blues Progression using 5 (Power) Chords:

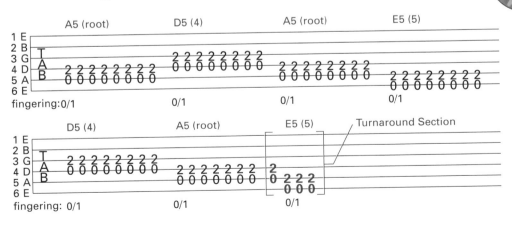

NOTE

You should be reminded of *Wild Thing* as you play this PROGRESSION. Pay attention to the number of strums each note gets.

"A" BLUES RIFF

A common BLUES RIFF is built on the Power Chords in each Blues Progression. To create this riff add the 6th note to each chord every other time.

A5 (Power Chord)

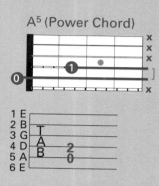

A6 (Interval)

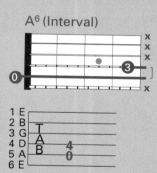

EXERCISE

TRACK 32

You can also play this Riff by leaving your 1st finger on the fretboard. This will save you extra movement when playing this Riff.

Using the Blues Riff in the Blues Progression

Now apply the BLUES RIFF using the "A" Blues Progression.

TRACK 32

"A" Blues Progression with Riff

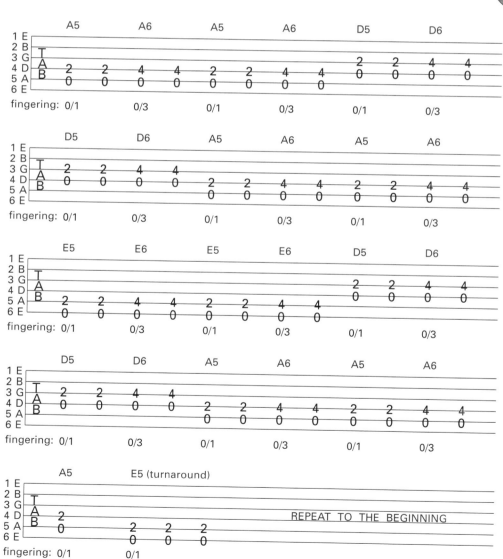

RED HOUSE

Jimi recorded this song in the key of "B♭." For your skill level we will transpose *Red House* down a half-step to the key of "A". This will allow you to utilize the skills you've learned earlier practicing the BLUES PROGRESSION.

Step 1

This song is a prime example of starting a BLUES-based song with a TURN-AROUND. The opening turnaround starts out on the 1st and 3rd strings, 9th fret. You will need to hold down the two strings with your 2nd and 3rd fingers or BAR the 1st, 2nd, and 3rd string with your 3rd finger.

TRACK 33

With your picking hand, play back and forth between the 3rd and 1st strings.

Here is the opening RIFF of *Red House:*

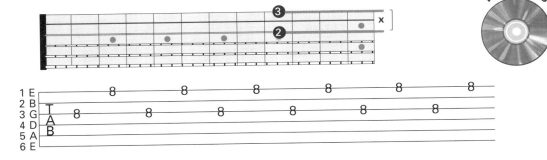

Step 2

This is the same riff, but it's moved down to the 8th fret.

TRACK 33

Red House is a BLUES- based composition that is perfect for practicing your new skills. By practicing *Red House*, you will learn the following:

1. The key of "A".
2. The Root, 4, 5, Blues Progression.
3. The Blues Riff.
4. "A" Blues Turn-around.
5. Musical rests.
6. "A" Major Third Interval.
7. One of Jimi Hendrix's greatest hits!

Step 3

Now move back to the 9th fret and play both strings at the same time. (Note: The middle string is muted. To mute the string, barely lay your 2nd finger across the top.)

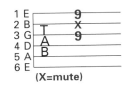

(X=mute)

TRACK 33

Step 4

This next section is where Jimi takes off with one of his classic BLUES LEAD LICKS. We haven't yet covered the scales he uses, so for now REST for seven counts by counting: **1, 2, 3, 4, 5, 6, 7**

(When you count in music, pronounce "seven" as "sen" so you don't accidentally count to eight.)

RED HOUSE *(continued)*

Step 5

Here is the part of the song where you get to practice the Blues (root, 4, 5) Progression with the open POWER CHORDS. You will be playing the rhythm guitar part of this song, so as you listen to the song, try to

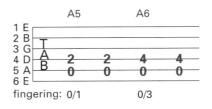

concentrate on the rhythm guitar that's in the background of Jimi's solo. (Note: this is the same Blues Progression you played on pages 40, 41, 42.)

Here is the complete verse using the blues riff within the root, 4, 5, progression of "A" (notice we start on the 4 (D) of the progression):

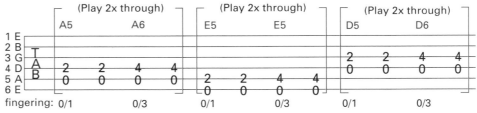

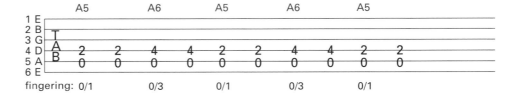

THEORY

D Major 3rd Interval or Chord

The 1st (root) and 3rd notes of a major scale are called the "Major 3rd interval."

D Major Scale:

(root)	2	3	4	5	6	7
D	E	F#	G	A	B	C#

D Major 3rd Interval:

(root)	3rd
D	F#

Step 6

There are two intervals that end the verse of the Blues Progression. In this song, Jimi uses the D# and E Major 3rd (interval) chords (see side-bar).

Use your 1st and 2nd fingers to play the major 3rd chords, sliding (one half-step up) both fingers to the next frets.

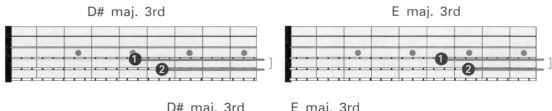

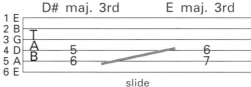

Step 1

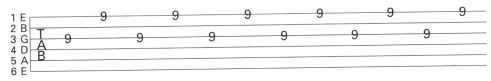

Step 2

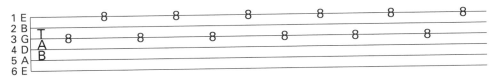

Step 3

Step 4

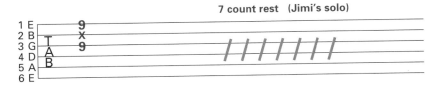

7 count rest   (Jimi's solo)

TRACK 35

Step 5

VERSE

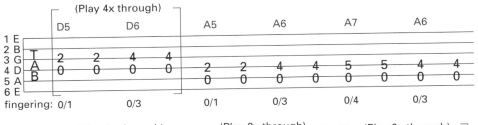

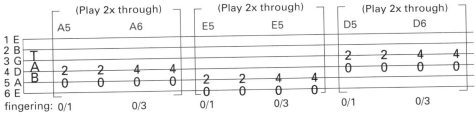

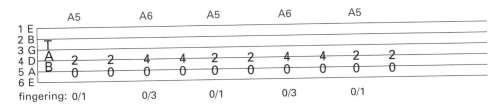

Step 6

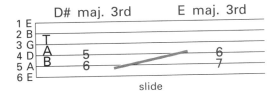

D# maj. 3rd   E maj. 3rd

slide

45

MAJOR CHORDS (OPEN)

WOW, check out all the notes! The "E" Major scale on the right is extended over two octaves in a vertical pattern on the guitar neck, so we have the same notes, only more of them. There's no need to focus on this right now; the most important thing is the "E" Major chord which we'll build from this scale.

Below, look for the ROOT notes and OCTAVES (E).

"E" Major Scale:

E	F#	G#	A	B	C#	D#	E
(root)	2	3	4	5	6	7	(octave)

Notes on guitar grid:

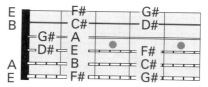

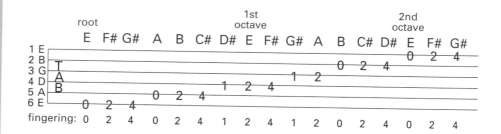

Major Chord Formula

(root)   3   5

"E" Major Scale and Chord Formula

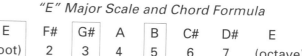

E	F#	G#	A	B	C#	D#	E
(root)	2	3	4	5	6	7	(octave)

"E" Major Chord (notes)

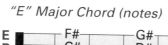

"E" Major Chord (fingering)

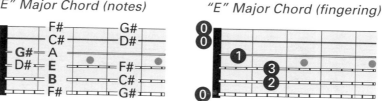

TRACK 36

Chord Guidelines

When building a chord from an extended scale, consider the following guidelines:

1. Establish which lower string the root note is to be built from. The string containing the root note will usually be the first string you strum.

2. The other notes of the chord are established on the higher strings (below the root on the guitar neck). The root, 3rd, and 5th notes don't need to be in a specific order, but all the notes must be included in the chord. The root, 3rd, and 5th notes can be a combination from any of the octaves of the extended scale, and they do not all have to fall within the same octave.

3. Practice placing your fingers in their positions one at a time (1st finger, then 2nd finger, then 3rd, etc.) when adjusting to play a chord. As your technique develops, you'll be able to move all your fingers simultaneously for chord changes.

Take a moment to think about the formula for building chords (page 24). Earlier we used the key of "A" Major, but now we can apply the formula to the "E" Major scale.

NOTE

These chords are hard on your fingers at first. Be patient! With practice your fingers will toughen up and, before you know it, these chords will be easy. Soon you'll be playing all kinds of songs!

MINOR CHORDS (OPEN)

The OPEN MINOR CHORD is derived from the same formula as the OPEN MAJOR CHORD with only subtle differences. The minor chord is built off of the MINOR SCALE. Remember that you FLAT (b) the 3rd, 6th, and 7th notes (move each down a half-step) of a major scale to convert it to a minor scale (page 20).

"E" Minor Scale:

E	F#	G	A	B	C	D	E
(root)	2	b3	4	5	b6	b7	(octave)

Notes on guitar grid:

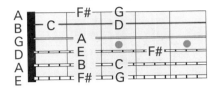

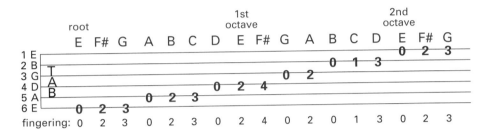

Minor Chord Formula

(root)	b3	b5

"E" Minor Scale

E	F#	G	A	B	C	D	E
(root)	2	b3	4	5	b6	b7	(octave)

"E" Minor Chord (notes)

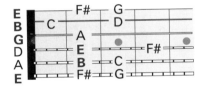

"E" Minor Chord (fingering)

TRACK 37

4. Changing chords will be a slow, painful struggle at first. Practice, practice, and practice the chord changes again until you feel comfortable with them.

5. When picking or strumming a chord, be sure not to play any strings that are excluded from the chord. Many times you can use your fret fingers to mute these excess strings.

6. Before you pick all the strings at once to play your chord, play each string individually to be sure all the notes of your chord are ringing correctly and the desired strings are not accidentally muted.

7. To avoid muting strings, pay attention to how you place your fingers on the fretboard and correct any bad habits right away. Your fingers should stand almost perpendicular to the fretboard, not lay flat across the strings (unless you are intentionally muting the strings).

In this book there is a chord reference section (page 64) for you to study. In addition, I suggest you purchase a chord dictionary to have for your reference.

CHORDS

IMPORTANT NOTE

Remember that OCTAVES are basically the same notes, only higher. This is why we are able to play all six strings with these chords.

NOTE

Make sure your fingers don't MUTE strings as you press on the desired FRET.

NOTE

There are several tricks to remember when shifting from one chord to the next:

- Sometimes you can leave one or more fingers in place, simply moving a single finger into the new position.

- Sometimes you can simply slide a finger into the new position.

- Sometimes you can move your finger to the lowest bass string first. (This gives you a half a second to place your other fingers before you strum the appropriate strings.) Try this shifting from D to G.

OPEN CHORDS

In this section we will learn four new OPEN CHORDS. To make the learning process more interesting, we will apply them to a familiar song.

"G" Major Chord

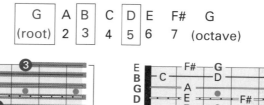

"D" Major Chord

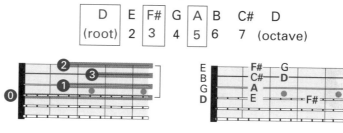

"C" Major Chord

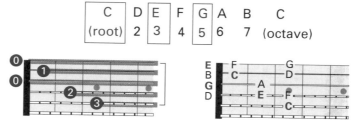

"A" Minor Chord

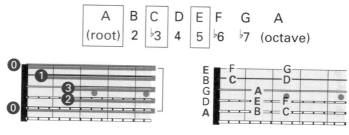

Notice that the "C" Major and "A" Minor scales consist of the same notes. They are considered to be RELATIVE SCALES (i.e., same notes, different order). This concept will be covered in detail in later books.

KNOCKIN' ON HEAVEN'S DOOR

As far as I know, Jimi has never performed Bob Dylan's *Knockin' on Heaven's Door*. I decided to include this song in the book anyway because it has a chord structure you can now play. It is one of my personal favorite Dylan songs other than *All Along the Watchtower*.

You will use the chords that you learned earlier: "G" major, "D" major, "C" major and "A" minor.

Rhythm Charts

Knockin' on Heaven's Door has been written (below) using a method called RHYTHM CHARTS. This method of writing is illustrated on the staff (covered later in this book) with RHYTHM BARS that represent which chord is to be strummed for each beat. The chord name is given just above the staff, directly above the rhythm bar that designates a chord change.

KNOCKIN' ON HEAVEN'S DOOR

Verse (repeat 4 times)

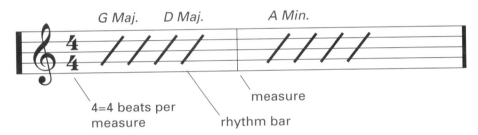

Note: Each rhythm bar represents one beat.

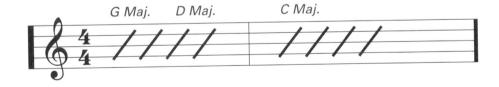

CHORD GRIDS

In most guitar song and reference books, the CHORD GRIDS stand vertically. To help you adjust, we will convert to this standard throughout the rest of this book.

"E" Minor Chord (fingering)

Here is the diagram you just learned:

Here is the standard we will convert to; the view is like standing your guitar on your lap and looking up on the guitar neck.

49

READING MUSIC

Staff, Notes, Rests, Timing, Etc.

In this section you'll learn the basics of reading staff notation, sheet music, and song books. Understanding these concepts is essential to the development of your music skills.

Step 1—The Staff

The STAFF is a means of designating the pitch and name of a note. Notice that the staff consists of 5 lines and 4 spaces. Here are the names of the notes that each position represents.

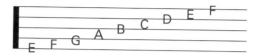

Step 2— Treble Clef

The TREBLE CLEF indicates the music is written for high register instruments (guitar, flute, etc.). This sign is also known as the "G" clef, because the sign encircles the "G" note on the staff.

Step 3—Measures

The staff line is broken into MEASURES to help you keep track of the BEATS of the music.

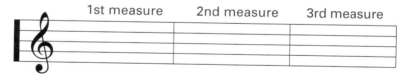

Step 4—Time Signature

The TIME SIGNATURE lets you know how many BEATS or counts per measure. In this example the music is in 4/4 time (or 4 beats per measure). Most ROCK songs are in 4/4 time.

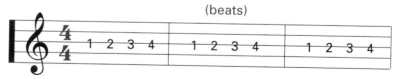

Time signatures are not always in 4/4 time. Here are two more variations, one in 3/4 time (which has a "waltz" feel to it), and the other in 2/4 time:

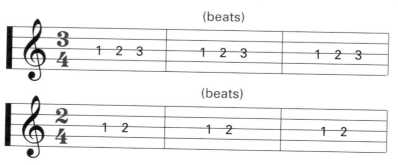

You can remember the *lines* by memorizing this phrase:

Every
Good
Boy
Deserves
Fudge

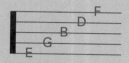

You can remember the *lines* by memorizing this word:

FACE

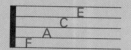

Step 5—Note Duration (how long notes sustain)

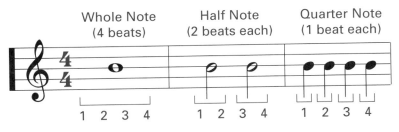

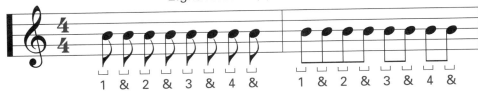

Eighth notes can be single with a flag ♪ or attached together with a beam ▬ .

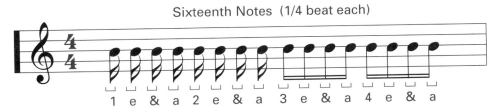

Above is a method of counting beats.

Sixteenth notes can be single with two flags or attached with a double beam.

Dotted Notes—adding a dot to a note adds half of the original value to the total duration.

Tied Notes—Tied notes are 2 notes of the same pitch combined together to increase the note duration. It is now equal to the duration of both notes.

Rests—Rests are silent spots common in all music. Each rest sign has an equal value to the notes you have learned earlier.

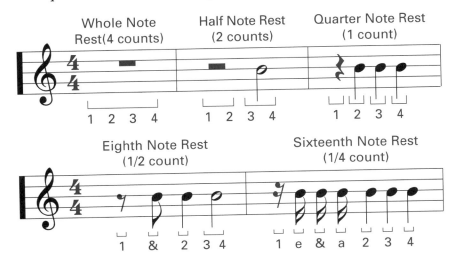

51

READING MUSIC *(continued)*

Ledger Lines

The guitar's musical range is wider than the staff allows. Ledger lines are the extensions of the staff allowing you to read or write these notes.

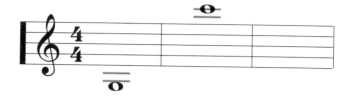

Repeat Signs

The repeat sign tells you to repeat a section of music. In this example, you play

the notes starting from measure 1 up to the repeat sign (measure 3). Then you return to measure 1 to repeat the three measures one time.

First and Second Endings

First and second endings indicate you should play all the way through the first ending, return to the beginning, and play through the second ending (skipping the first ending this time).

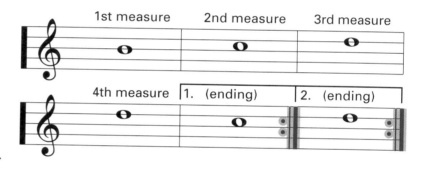

Accidentals

Accidentals raise or lower a note in pitch. The *sharp* (#) sign RAISES the note one-half step (one fret), and the *flat* (♭) sign LOWERS the note one-half step (one fret).

Ascending

Notice the note is on the same line as the "F", but there is a sharp sign (#) next to it.

Descending

The F# and G♭ are the same note; the name depends on which KEY the note is in and the direction it is moving (up or down a half-step).

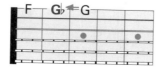

Natural Sign

The natural sign (♮) is used to restore a sharp or flat note to its original pitch.

When an ACCIDENTAL is placed in a measure, it affects all notes of the same pitch (or octave) that occur after that note for the rest of the measure only. This saves labeling all of the notes to show they are accidentals.

Example:

The NATURAL SIGN has the same effect on a measure as the accidentals above. This sign will convert all the notes of the same pitch or octave within a measure.

Example:

EXERCISE 1

Write down the names for each of these notes:

EXERCISE 2

Write down the names for each of these notes:

ANSWERS:
Exercise One— G G E F# G E F# F# G F# F E F#
Exercise Two— F# F# F F E E F F F# F# F F E E F E F#

53

READING EXERCISES

1st String (E)

Here are some exercises for you to practice your reading skills. You'll start with the high "E" string and progress from there. The first 3 notes you will use are:

TRACK 41

EXERCISE 1

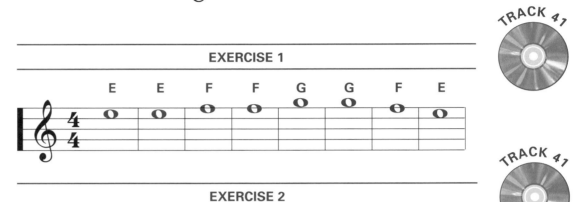

TRACK 41

EXERCISE 2

TRACK 41

EXERCISE 3

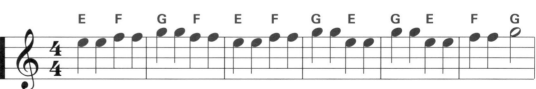

TRACK 41

EXERCISE 4

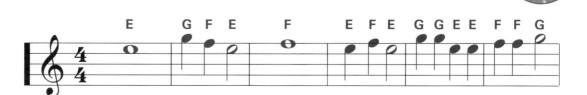

Note: More exercises available online at
http://www.jimi-hendrix.com

54

2nd String (B)

Here are the notes for the "B" string:

EXERCISE 1

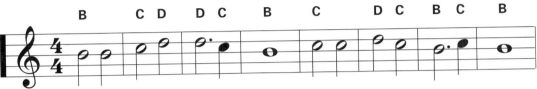

EXERCISE 2

TWO STRING (E & B) COMPOSITIONS—EXERCISE 1

TWO STRING (E & B) COMPOSITIONS—EXERCISE 2

This is a simplified version of the opening melody in *Crosstown Traffic*.

READING EXERCISES *(continued)*

3rd String (G)

Here are the notes on your "G" string.

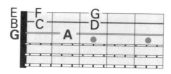 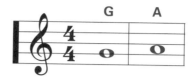 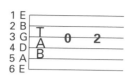

TRACK 43

EXERCISE 1

3rd String (G)

Here are the accidental notes on your "G" string.

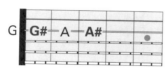 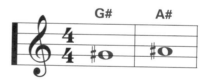 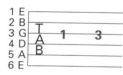

TRACK 43

EXERCISE 2

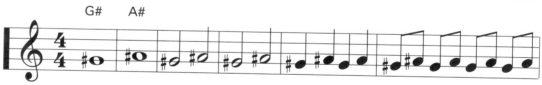

 Note: More exercises available online at
http://www.jimi-hendrix.com

56

BURNING THE MIDNIGHT LAMP

The Introduction to *Burning the Midnight Lamp* is an excellent melody to practice reading the "E" and "B" strings. This melody includes notes on the 5th and 6th strings, but they are only an optional part of the exercise for now. The song has been transposed up on OCTAVE so you can practice reading the notes you have learned so far.

Here are the notes you will play in this song.

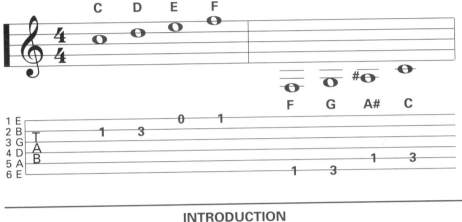

TRACK 44

INTRODUCTION

The part you are playing is actually the harpsichord that plays along with the guitar melody. If you don't play the guitar part in greyscale (on the 5th and 6th strings), be sure to rest for one count on each note.

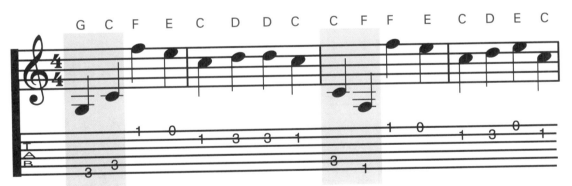

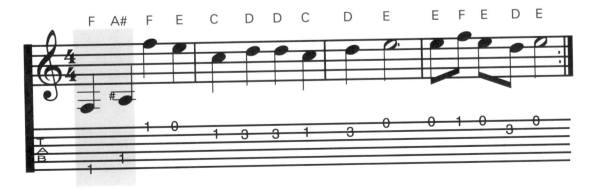

STAR SPANGLED BANNER

TRACK 45

Jimi played the *Star Spangled Banner* in the key of "E" major. Let's go through the "E" major scale to help you see and practice the notes used in this song.

The version of *Star Spangled Banner* below, is of the original song. Due to the advanced techniques (trills, hammer-ons, pull-offs, feedback, etc.) Jimi uses, it would be difficult at this stage of your development to illustrate.

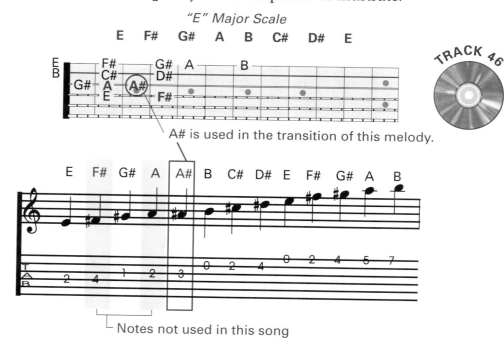

"E" Major Scale

A# is used in the transition of this melody.

Notes not used in this song

TRACK 46

KEY SIGNATURE

The KEY SIGNATURE of a song can be shown by placing a sharp (#) or flat (b) at the beginning of the staff. In the example below, every "F" in the song is sharped (#). Key signatures are used so that the ACCIDENTAL does not need to be written before every sharped or flatted note.

Here is the fingering position for the beginning of the song. It may look tough, but notice that it is simply built off the "E" Major chord.

TRACK 46

PART ONE— Intro.

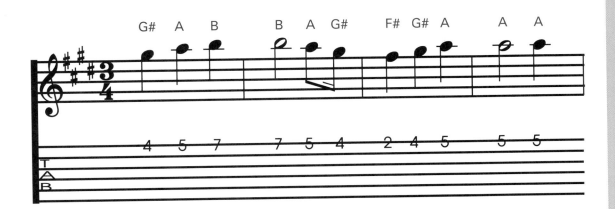

PART TWO

"E" Minor Pentatonic Scale

This is a common scale used by Jimi in both his songs and solos. We will be using this scale in *Purple Haze*.

Pentatonic refers to the number 5. Notice there are only 5 different notes in this scale.

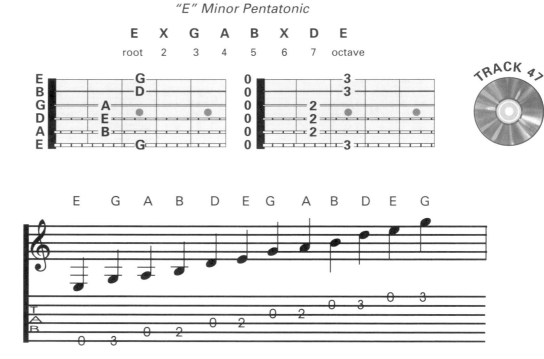

"E" Minor Pentatonic

TRACK 47

PURPLE HAZE

Purple Haze is a perfect song to challenge you on techniques that we've covered in this book. This song will help you to prepare and understand future song books. *Purple Haze* brings together such techniques as octaves, lead riffs, and other related elements.

TRACK 48

Step 1—Introduction (octaves)

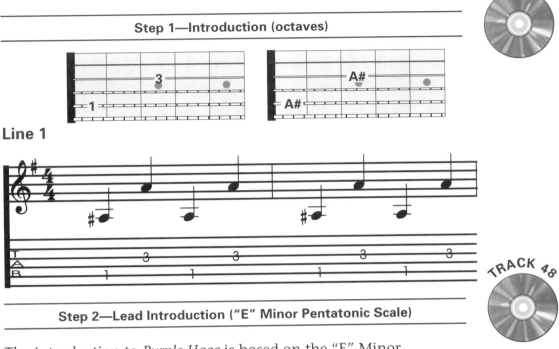

Line 1

TRACK 48

Step 2—Lead Introduction ("E" Minor Pentatonic Scale)

The introduction to *Purple Haze* is based on the "E" Minor Pentatonic Scale. Here are the notes that you will use in the opening lead riff:

"E" Minor Pentatonic Scale

Suggested fingering

Line 2 B D G A A G D E E E

(slide) (slight bend)

Line 3 B D G A A G D E E D

(slide) (slight bend)

NOTE

The notes you are playing for *Purple Haze* are authentic, but the position on the guitar neck has been adjusted to accommodate for the scales that we have been working on. This transcription has also been subtly adjusted for your skill level.

61

PURPLE HAZE *(continued)*

Line 4

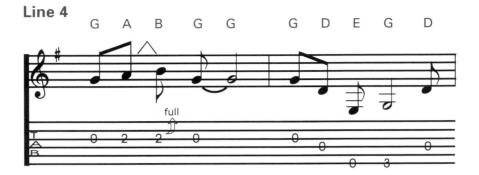

Line 5

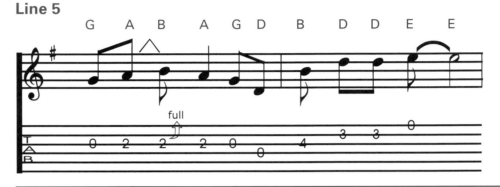

Step 3—Verse

The verse of *Purple Haze* is based on an
E7#9 chord. The version of the chord
you'll play is exactly the same as the part
you played earlier in *Foxey Lady*.

We will only use a portion of this chord.

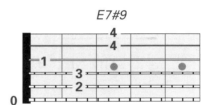

E7#9

Line 7

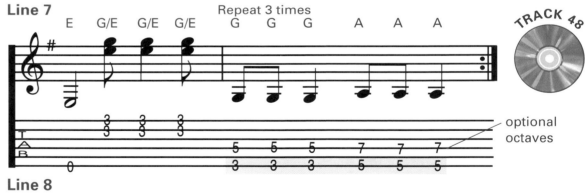

Line 8

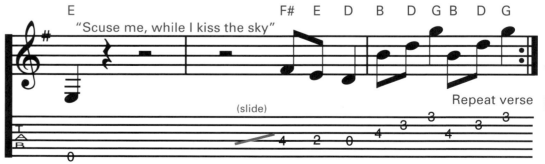

JAM WITH JIMI

CHARTS

Guitar Neck Note Chart

In this chart you can refer to any note on the guitar neck and all its related notes.

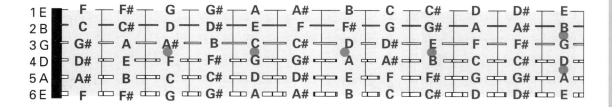

Guitar Staff Chart

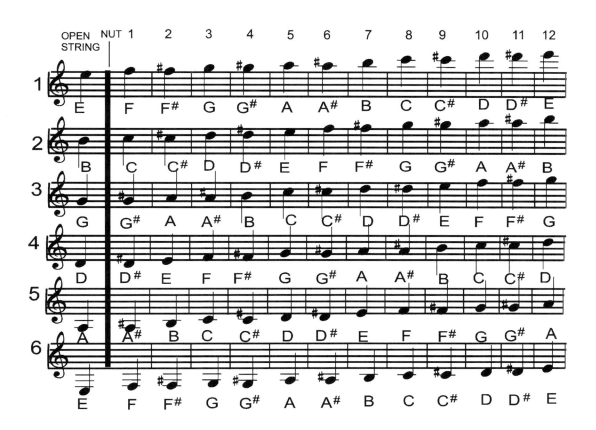

Guitar Chord Chart

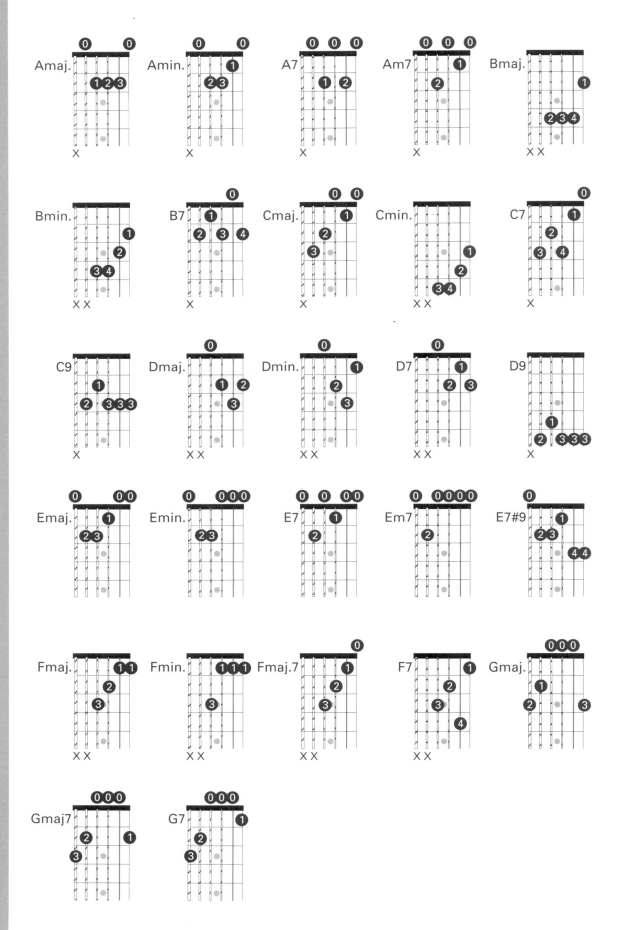